MW00912850

Table of Contents

Introduction

Smoking meats is not a new art. The concept of smoking meat dates back to caveman days when it was necessary for preserving food. As years went by, smoking meat became a popular form of preserving meats for a later date.

Today, meat is smoked to add flavor and carry through with a historically its delicious trend. There are three main types of smoking meat, cold smoking, hot smoking, and smoke roasting.

Cold smoking is used as a flavor enhancer for items such as chicken breasts, beef, pork chops, and salmon, scallops, it and steak. Cold smoking is used for a short duration of time to add flavor to foods that are baked, grilled, steamed, it or sautéed before eating.

Hot smoking exposes the meat to a low, and controlled temperature for a long duration of time. Foods that are hot snow are typically save to eat without further cooking, as long as the internal temperature reaches the recommended degrees Fahrenheit listed by the FDA.

Smoked roasting is a process that refers to smoking combined with either roasting or baking. This smoking message is typically referred to as barbecuing, it baking, or pit roasting. It is typically done over a smoke roast, closed wood fire, or barbecued grill. Essentially, as long as you have a fire and wood chips, and the temperature can RE above 250° F, you can smoke almost any type of meat.

We hope you enjoyed these 25 delicious "Smoked Meat" recipes, and we hope you share them with your family and friends.

Smoking Meats

Smoking meats may take a long time, but this is because while you are cooking meat at a low temperature and slowly in this fashion brings out the true flavor and tender nature of the meat. It can even make toughest cuts of meat succulent and juicy.

There is no reason to spend top dollar on expensive cuts of meat when you can easily smoke a tough brisket and create an amazing work of art for dinner. With the art of smoking meat, even the least appealing of meats can become amazingly tender and deliciously juicy. If you can do this with an unappealing cut of meat, just imagine what you can do with a top quality piece of meat like a Boston butt roast or a gorgeous beef roast.

Even if you have not enjoyed the wonderful flavor of smoked meat before, we guarantee that you will be instantly hooked and it smoking will become a regular part of your family's life. You will be hosting backyard barbecues in no time!

Smoked Cedar Plank Salmon
(ready in about 30 minutes | Serving 1)

Ingredients:

- 4 tbsp vegetable oil
- 6 tbsp bourbon
- 2 tbsp soy sauce
- 1 tsp ground ginger
- 2 tbsp light brown sugar
- Ground black pepper, to taste
- 2 pound fillet of salmon
- 1 tsp fresh squeezed lemon juice

Directions:

1. In a medium bowl, combine all of your dry ingredients. In another bowl, blend wet ingredients. Mix together to create marinade.
2. Remove any pin bones that the butcher left in the salmon fillet.
3. Place the salmon in a shallow dish or bowl. Pour marinade over the salmon and allow to sit covered with saran wrap for at least 20 minutes.
4. Preheat your cedar plank while your fillet marinades. When your plank is preheated, lift the lid and place the fish skin side down on the plan. Place the lid back on the hot smoker for about 10 minutes, or until the fillet is done to your specifications.
5. Transfer the marinade into a small sauce pan. Bring the mixture to a simmer and allow it to reduce to ½ of what it originally started as. Remove the glaze from the heat and add in lemon juice. Drizzle the mixture over the salmon right before serving.

Smooth-Smoked Ham
(ready in about 5 hours | Serving 12)

Ingredients:

- 1 cured ham
- 1 cup mustard
- Spices to your liking
- Hickory wood chips

Directions:

1. Apply the mustard in a thin layer over the outside of the ham. Rub on any spice mix you may want making sure to cover the ham entirely.
2. Heat smoker to 225 degrees °F and apply hickory wood chips. Wait till the smoker begins to smoke.
3. Place the ham in the smoker and let smoke for 3 to 5 hours.

Apple Smoked Spare Ribs
(ready in about 6 hours | Serving 6)

Ingredients:

- 2 slabs pork spareribs
- ½ tsp. ground cloves
- ½ tsp. cinnamon
- Apple wood chips
- 1/4th tsp. pepper

Barbeque sauce
- ½ cup molasses
- 2 (15 oz.) cans tomato sauce

- 2 tbsp. ground cumin
- 10 cloves garlic
- Fresh ground pepper
- 2 tbsp. dry mustard
- 1/4th tsp. hot pepper flakes
- ½ tsp cinnamon
- ½ cup red wine vinegar

Directions:

1. Rub down the ribs with the cloves pepper and cinnamon on both sides. Place the ribs on the smoking rack
2. Smoke ribs in the smoker for 6 hours with apple wood chips until tender or internal temp of 170 degrees °F.
3. Mix in all the barbeque sauce ingredients and simmer on low heat, covered for 1 hour. Stir occasionally while adding vinegar to taste. Allow to simmer for 15 additional minutes. Place in the refrigerator until cool.

Simple Smoked Chicken
(ready in about 6 hours | Serving 8)

Ingredients:

- Chicken 3 to 3.5 lb.
- 1 gallon water
- Oak wood chips
- 1 cup sugar
- 1 cup salt
- Any other spices or liquid sauces you may want to add.

Directions:

1. Place the salt, sugar and any other spices you may want in the gallon of water. Place the chicken in the water and let sit for 4 hours. Remove the chicken and rinse the brine off.
2. You can now season your chicken any way you want and place in a smoker breast side down, holding a temperature of 225 °F with oak chips as a wood base.
3. Place hickory in on the oak to give it more flavor. Cook the chicken for 1 ½ hours. Remove the chicken when internal temperature reaches 140 °F.

Deep Smoked Meatloaf
(ready in about 4 hours | Serving 8)

Ingredients:

- 2 lbs. ground beef
- ½ green pepper, finely chopped
- 1 onion, chopped finely
- 1 cup bread crumbs
- 2 cloves garlic, minced
- 3/4th cup ketchup
- 2 eggs lightly beaten
- 1/4th cup milk

Directions:

1. Blend all ingredients into a bowl until well mixed. Place the mixture on a cookie sheet and mold into a form.
2. Place in the smoker with any flavored wood chips you want at 250 °F for 3 to 4 hours. Add ketchup or barbeque sauce the last 30 minutes before finishing. Make sure the internal temperature registers at 150 °F.

Grand Texas Smoked Brisket
(ready in about 1 ½ day | Serving 8 to 10)

Ingredients:

- Wood chips of your flavor
- 1/4th cup sugar
- 1/4th cup paprika
- 1/4th cup cayenne pepper
- 1/4th cup ground cumin
- 1/4th cup chili powder
- 1/4th cup brown sugar
- 1/4th cup onion powder
- 1/4th cup garlic powder
- 1/4th cup fresh cracked black pepper
- 1/4th cup salt

- 10 lbs. of beef brisket

Directions:

1. Place wood chips in a bowl with water to soak for 8 hours.
2. In a bowl mix sugar, paprika, cayenne pepper, cumin, chili powder, brown sugar, onion powder, garlic powder, black pepper and salt together.
3. Preheat your smoker at 220 F°. Drain the water from your wood chips and place them in your smoker.
4. Place the brisket in the smoker and let smoke for 12 ½ hours or until the temperature inside reaches 165 °F. Remove and wrap tightly in heavy-duty aluminum foil. Return the brisket to the smoker.
5. Cook for an additional 1 hour or until internal temperature reaches 185 °F

Prime Maple-Smoked Rib
(ready in about 1 hour 30 minutes | Serving 5 to 6)

Ingredients:

- 1 (6 lb.) rib roast, 3 rib standing, bones separated and tied back in place.
- 3 cups maple wood chips
- Sea salt to taste
- Coarse ground black pepper to taste

Directions:

1. Place wood chips in a bowl of water for 1 hour until moistened completely.

2. Preheat your smoker to be 225 °F and hang the drip pan on the rack beneath the area where the meat will be.
3. Coat the roast with salt and pepper working it in with your hands.
4. Place the roast fat side up into the preheated smoker.
5. Place 2/3 cup of the wood chips into the smoker
6. Smoke the roast for 30 minutes and add half of the wood chips that are remaining. Smoke for 30 more minutes and add the last half of the wood chips. Smoke for about 2 more hours or until the internal temperature reaches 125 °F.
7. Remove the roast and let it rest for 30 minutes before carving ½ to 1 inch thick slices.

Smoked Pork Spare Ribs
(ready in about 12 hours | Serving 6)

Ingredients:

- 2 Tbsps. Chili powder
- ½ cup packed brown sugar
- 1 tbsp. black pepper
- 1 tbsp. paprika
- 2 tsp. onion powder
- 2 tbsps. Garlic powder
- 2 tsps. Ground cumin
- 2 tsps. Salt
- 1 tsp. jalapeno seasoning salt
- 1 tsp. ground cinnamon
- 1 tsp. cayenne pepper

- ¾ cup apple cider vinegar
- 1 cup apple cider
- 1 tbsp. garlic powder
- 1 tbsp. onion powder
- 1 jalapeno pepper, finely chopped
- 2 tbsps. Lemon juice
- Kosher salt and ground black pepper to taste
- 3 tbsps. Hot pepper sauce
- 2 cups wood chips, soaked
- 6 lbs. pork spareribs

Directions:

1. Mix the first 11 ingredients in a bowl together and rub the mixture on the spare ribs. Make sure to coat them completely, cover and refrigerate for 4 hours.
2. Preheat your charcoal grill for 250 °F.
3. In a medium bowl mix the remaining ingredients not including the ribs.
4. Place 2 handfuls of wood chips on the now grayed charcoal. Lay the ribs out on the grill bone down. Close the grill and cook for 3 ½ to 4 hours. Add additional coals as you need them. Baste the ribs with the sauce and add a handful of woodchips every hour. Try to keep the temperature of the grill above 225 °F. The ribs will be done when the seasoning has become crispy and blackened. Also the meat will have pulled away from the bone

Carolina-Style Pulled Pork
(ready in about 15 hours | Serving 10)

Ingredients:

- 2 tsps. Light brown sugar
- 1 tbsp. mild paprika
- ½ tsp. celery salt
- 1 ½ tsps. hot paprika
- ½ tsp. dry mustard
- ½ tsp. garlic salt
- ½ tsp. onion powder

- ½ tsp. ground black pepper
- ¼ tsp. salt
- 1 1/3rd cups water
- 2 cups cider vinegar
- ¼ cup firmly packed brown sugar
- 5/8th cup ketchup
- 4 tsps. Crushed red pepper flakes
- 5 tsps. Salt
- 1 tsp. ground white pepper
- 1 tsp. ground black pepper.
- 2 lbs. hickory wood chips, soaked
- 8 lbs. pork butt roast

Directions:

1. Mix the first 9 ingredients into a small bowl and rub all over the roast. Wrap the roast in plastic wrap and refrigerate for 8 hours.
2. Preheat the grill at 225 °F and wait until coals become grayed over. When the coals gray over place a handful of wood chips on them. Place the pork butt roast on the grill over the drip pan. Close the grill and cook for 12 hours adding a handful of wood chips every hour. Also add coal as needed.
3. While the pork butt is smoking mix the last 8 ingredients not including the pork butt and wood chips into a medium bowl. Whisk the ingredients until they turn brown.
4. Remove the pork butt roast and start shredding. When the pork is shredded mix it in with the sauce you created

Smokehouse Beef Jerky
(ready in about 14 hours | Serving 1 lb.)

Ingredients:

- 1 cup Worcestershire sauce
- 2 cups soy sauce
- 1 cup teriyaki sauce
- 1 cup cranberry-grape juice
- 2 tbsp. steak sauce
- 1 tbsp. hot pepper sauce
- ½ tsp. ground black pepper, to taste
- 1 cup light brown sugar
- 4 cups wood chips, or as needed

- 2 lbs. flank steak, sliced into ¼ inch slices against the grain

Directions:

1. Whisk the first 8 ingredients together and pour into a reseal able plastic bag. Place the sliced meat in the bag and press out the air before sealing it. Place the bag in the refrigerator and let it marinade for 8 to 10 hours.
2. With the smoker at 170 °F, remove the slices of steak and place on the rack of the smoker and add the wood chips. Smoke for about 6 to 8 hours adding a handful of wood chips every hour.

Smoked Citrus Goose Breast
(ready in about 4 hours | Serving 8)

Ingredients:

- 1/3 cup olive oil
- ½ cup orange juice
- 1/3 cup brown sugar
- 1/3 cup Dijon mustard
- 1/4th cup soy sauce
- 1/4th cup honey
- 1 tsp. garlic powder
- 1 tbsp. dried minced onion
- 1 cup hickory wood chips, soaked
- 8 goose breast halves

Directions:

1. Whisk all the ingredients together in a large bowl. Cover the bowl and place in the refrigerator for 3 to 6 hours
2. Preheat the smoker to around 300 °F and when it reaches its peak add a handful of hickory wood chips.
3. Place the goose on the smoker grate and brush on the marinade every couple minutes for the first 30 minutes. Cook until the internal temperature reaches 165 °F.

Smoked Hot Wings

(ready in about 2 hours 30 minutes | Serving 9)

Ingredients:

- 4 tbsps. Cajun seasoning
- 2 tbsps. Butter
- 4 cups vegetable oil
- 16 oz. hot sauce

Directions:

1. Preheat your smoker to 200 °F and place 1 cup of the wood chips in to begin smoking.

2. Use 2 tbsps. Of the Cajun seasoning to coat the chicken wings
3. Place the wings on the smoker grate and add another handful of wood chips. Begin smoking the wings for 2 hours.
4. In a large pan mix garlic, butter, and 2 tbsps. Cajun seasoning on medium-low heat. Cook the mixture down until butter is melted while stirring. Pour in the hot sauce and stir until mixed. Simmer the hot sauce stirring it occasionally until sauce has thickened.
5. Heat up oil in your deep-fryer to 375 °F
6. Preheat the grill to 375 °F
7. Cook your wings in batches of 10 to 12 in the deep fryer. When they are cooked through and lightly browned remove, drain and place on a baking sheet. Baste each wing with the hot sauce mixture.
8. Place the sauced wings on the grill cooking the wings so that the sauce has caramelized and become crisp.

Smoked Stealhead Trout

(ready in about 13 hours | Serving 6)

Ingredients:

- 2 tbsps. Olive oil
- 2 lbs. steelhead trout fillets
- 1 ½ tbsps. rosemary, crushed
- 4 cloves garlic, chopped
- 1 quart water
- 1 cup sugar-based curing mixture
- 1 lb. alder wood chips, soaked in water
- Ground black pepper to taste

Directions:

1. Place the fish fillets in a glass baking dish after rinsing them off. Drizzle your olive oil on top of the fish and season with rosemary and garlic. Rub the fish down with seasonings, cover and place in and refrigerate overnight.
2. Mix the curing salt into the water until dissolved and pour it in with the fish. Let the curing agent sit for 15 minutes for every half inch the thickness of the fish.
3. Preheat your smokers temperature to 150 °F
4. Remove your fish from the curing mixture, discarding the liquid. Place each fish fillet on an individual aluminum foil sheet just big enough for the fillet. Season the fillet with pepper to taste. Place 1 handful of soaked wood chips in the smoker and cover for 2 hours allowing the fish to smoke. Place another handful 1 hour through.
5. Raise the heat of the smoker to 200 °F and smoke the fish until the temperature inside of the fish is 165 °F Remove and let the fillet rest for 20 minutes.

Rich Smoked Maple Bacon
(ready in about 5 days | Serving 1)

Ingredients:

- 2 tbsps. Sodium nitrate
- 1 ½ gallons water
- 2 cups salt
- 1 cup sugar-based curing mixture
- ½ cup maple syrup
- 1 cup packed brown sugar
- Maple wood chips

Directions:

1. Mix sodium nitrate, water, coarse salt, curing salt, maple syrup, and brown sugar into a large pot on high heat. Bring to a boil and cook for 10 to 15 minutes dissolving everything completely. Pour 5 gallons of brine into a plastic bucket and allow 6 to 8 hours for it to cool to room temperature.
2. Cut 4 to 6 slabs of pork belly against the grain and leaving the skin on to fit in the bucket and on your smoker. Place the pork in the brine and hold under the solution for 5 to 7 days while refrigerated. Make sure to mix the mixture and the pork around daily.
3. Remove and rinse the brine solution off while rubbing the pork to get any extra off. Dry off the pork and place on the smoker for about 2 hours until the surface begins to dry.
4. Add a handful of maple wood chunks every hour with the cooking temperature of 110 °F. Smoke for around 8 to 12 hours

Smoked-Fennel Salmon
(ready in about 1 hour 45 minutes | Serving 1)

Ingredients:

- 4 tbsp vegetable oil
- 6 tbsp bourbon
- 2 tbsp soy sauce
- 1 tsp ground ginger
- 2 tbsp light brown sugar
- Ground black pepper, to taste
- 2 pound fillet of salmon
- 1 tsp fresh squeezed lemon juice

Directions:

1. In a medium bowl, combine all of your dry ingredients. In another bowl, blend wet ingredients. Mix together to create marinade.
2. Remove any pin bones that the butcher left in the salmon fillet.
3. Place the salmon in a shallow dish or bowl. Pour marinade over the salmon and allow to sit covered with saran wrap for at least 20 minutes.
4. Preheat your cedar plank while your fillet marinades. When your plank is preheated, lift the lid and place the fish skin side down on the plan. Place the lid back on the hot smoker for about 10 minutes, or until the fillet is done to your specifications.
5. Transfer the marinade into a small sauce pan. Bring the mixture to a simmer and allow it to reduce to ½ of what it originally started as. Remove the glaze from the heat and add in lemon juice. Drizzle the mixture over the salmon right before serving.

Comely Smoked Turkey
(ready in about 10 hours | Serving 1 10 lb. turkey)

Ingredients:

- 4 cloves garlic, crushed
- 1 (10 lb.) whole turkey, remove giblets and neck
- ½ cup butter
- 2 tbsps. Seasoned salt
- 1 apple, quartered
- 2 (12 fluid oz.) canned cola.
- 1 tbsp. garlic powder
- 1 onion, quartered
- 1 tbsp. ground black pepper
- 1 tbsp. salt

Directions:

1. Preheat your smoker to 225 °F
2. Rinse the turkey with cold water. Pat the turkey dry and rub the outside with crushed garlic. Sprinkle seasoned salt coating the outside of the turkey. Fill the cavity of the turkey with cola, butter, onion, apple, salt, garlic powder, and ground black pepper. Use foil to cover the cavity loosely.
3. Smoke the turkey for 10 hours basting every 1 to 2 hours. Measure the thickest part of the turkey to see if it has reached 180 °F.

Smoked Montreal Meat
(ready in about 53 hours 15 minutes | Serving 4 to 6)

Ingredients:

- 1 (3 to 5 lb.) brisket
- 6 oz. salt
- 1 gallon water
- 2 oz. powdered dextrose
- 2 oz. prague powder
- 2 ½ oz. pickling spices
- 4 tbsps. Pickling spices (brisket rub)

Directions:

1. IMix all the spices and water together in a large bowl. Submerge the brisket completely in brine. Allow to sit in the refrigerator for 2 days.
2. Remove the brisket from the bowl and rub down with 4 tbsps. Pickling spices
3. Place the brisket in the smoker with maple wood chips for 2 hours. Remove the brisket and sit in a pan filled with 2 cups of water. Wrap the pan and brisket with aluminum foil and place it in the oven for 3 hours at 250 °F
4. Remove the brisket from the oven and enjoy.

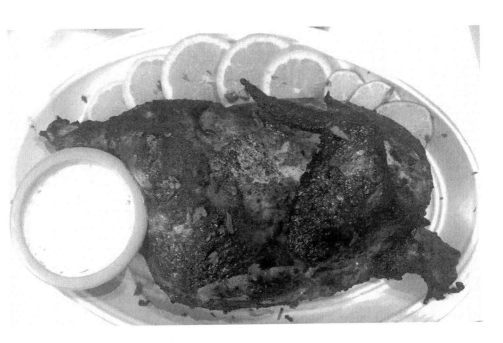

Smoked Chicken Mojo
(ready in about 6 hours | Serving 6)

Ingredients:

- 1 tbsp. orange zest
- 1/3 cup olive oil
- 1/3 cup fresh orange juice
- 1 tbsp. lime zest
- 1 bunch of cilantro, stems removed
- 1/4th cup lime juice
- 6 garlic cloves
- 1/4th cup oregano leaves
- 2 red jalapeno peppers, seeded
- 1 tsp. salt
- 1 1/4th tsp. ground cumin

- 6 chicken leg quarters
- 6 cups Applewood chips

Directions:

1. Place the first 12 ingredients into a processor and pulse for 20 seconds. Place ½ a cup of the mixture into the fridge to chill. Add the chicken into a large bowl along with the remaining of the mixture. Toss the chicken to coat with the mixture. Cover the chicken and place in the fridge to chill for 4 to 8 hours
2. Split the chips in half and wrap each half in heavy duty aluminum foil. Poke a hole in each one
3. Make sure one side of the grill is at 350 °F and leave the other unlit. Place on packet of the Applewood chips on the lit side with holes facing up.
4. Take the chicken out of the fridge and season with salt and pepper to your liking. Move the smoke pack to the side that is unlit and leave off the lid. Grill for 4 to 6 minutes on both sides. Place the smoke pack back to the lit side and recover. Cook for 1 hour and 30 minutes replacing the smoke packet half way through, turning the chicken occasionally. Make sure the internal temperature reaches 165 °F and remove from the grill. Let sit for 10 minutes and serve with leftover sauce.

Smoked Beef Brisket

(ready in about 12 hours 40 minutes | Serving 10 to 15)

Ingredients:

- 1 (12 to 14 lb.) beef brisket, trimmed
- 1 cup beef rub
- ½ cup Worcestershire sauce
- 3 to 4 pecan wood chunks
- Butcher paper
- Your choice of barbecue sauce
- 1 cup coarse ground black pepper
- 1 cup salt
- 2 tsps. Ground red pepper

- 3 tbsps. Garlic salt

Directions:

1. Baste the brisket with Worcestershire sauce. Cover the brisket with the beef rub and refrigerate for 1 to 4 hours.
2. Remove brisket and let sit for 1 hour. Set heat to 250 °F and place wood chunks to start smoking
3. Place the brisket on the grill fat side down. Cover and cook for 5 hours or until internal temperatures reach 165 °F. Remove and tightly wrap butcher paper around the brisket. Return the brisket to the smoker to cook for another 3 to 5 hours or center reaches 200 °F.
4. Remove the butcher paper wrapped brisket and open the paper. Let stand for 2 to 4 minutes. Loosely wrap back in paper and let stand for another 2 hours.

Wonderful Smoked Mussels
(ready in about 3 hours 30 minutes | Serving 4 lbs)

Ingredients:

- 4 lbs. mussels
- 1 cup water
- 1 cup white wine
- 1/4th cup olive oil
- Alder wood chunks

Directions:

1. Clean the mussels and add to covered boiling water in layers. Steam for about 3 minutes until they open. As you steam them all add the ones that have opened to a baking sheet.
2. Use a cheesecloth to strain the boiled water into a bowl and set to the side.
3. Using a small knife remove all the mussels from their shells. Cut the mussels beard off and add the cleaned mussel to the strained water. Soak the mussels for 20 minutes.
4. Preheat the smoker to 145 °F and add the alder wood chunks to get the smoke started. Using a fine grate, place the mussels in the smoker to smoke for around 2 hours.
5. Remove the mussels from the smoker and toss in oil and serve

Smoked Sturgeon
(ready in about 28 hours | Serving 5 lbs.)

Ingredients:

- 1 cup salt
- 3 to 5 lbs. of sturgeon, large cuts
- 1 tsp. mace
- 1/4th cup sugar
- Brandy
- 1 tbsp. garlic powder
- Wood chunks of choice

Directions:

1. Clean the sturgeon of any dark meat and fat. Coat the sturgeon with the mixture of sugar, salt, mace and garlic powder. Place the sturgeon on a bowl and place in the refrigerator to cure for 1 hour per pound of sturgeon.
2. Remove and rinse the sturgeon from the cure mixture. Dry the sturgeon by patting it with a paper towel. Brush on brandy covering the sturgeon completely. Move the sturgeon back to the fridge until the following day.
3. Preheat the smoker to 160 °F and add wood chunks to begin the smoking process. Place the sturgeon on the smoker and cover for 4 hours adding a handful of wood chunks every hour.
4. Remove and serve.

Smoked Beef Ribs
(ready in about 7 hours | Serving 6)

Ingredients:

- 1/4th cup brown sugar
- 1 tbsp. onion powder
- 1 tbsp. garlic powder
- 1 tbsp. black pepper
- 1 tbsp. salt
- 2 tsp. cumin
- 1 tbsp. chili powder
- 2 tsp. oregano
- 2 tsp. coriander
- ½ tsp. cayenne
- 1/4th tsp. thyme

- 1 bag wood chips, soaked in water
- 2 slabs of beef ribs

Directions:

1. Preheat your smoker to 225 °F
2. Use a knife to separate the membrane on the bottom of the ribs against the bone.
3. Mix all the seasoning together and completely coat the ribs top and bottom.
4. Place your wood chips on top of the coals and lay your ribs out on the grate bone side down.
5. Check the ribs every hour to see if the bone is sticking out a ½ an inch. This will tell you if the ribs are done.
6. Mop on barbecue sauce and place it sauce side down to caramelize the sauce.
7. Remove from the grill and let rest for ½ an hour.

Alabama Pig
(ready in about 1 day 12 hours | Serving 16)

Ingredients:

- 1/4th cup salt
- 3 cups apple cider vinegar
- 4 tbsp. ground black pepper
- 1/4th cup brown sugar
- 1/4th lb. butter
- 2 tbsp. cayenne pepper
- 5 lbs. Boston butt roast
- 1 qt. water

Directions:

1. Combine and mix salt, cider vinegar, black pepper, brown sugar, butter, and cayenne pepper in a saucepan. Place the pan over a medium-high heat and bring the ingredients to a rolling boil.
2. Preheat the smoker to 350 °F and place mesquite wood chips on top of the coals. Place the pork on the smoker basting with sauce every hour for 6 to 10 hours. Wrap the pork with aluminum foil adding sauce before closing tightly.
3. Place the meat back on the smoker for 2 hours. Check to see if the meat will pull away from the bone easily to tell if it is done.
4. Remove from the smoker and allow to cool. Pull the meat into large chunks
5. Place the chunks of meat in a pan. For every 4 lbs. of meat you need 1 cup of sauce. Mix and let sit to marinate.

Plank Smoked Salmon
(ready in about 10 hours 15 minutes | Serving 10)

Ingredients:

- Freshly ground black pepper to taste
- ½ tsp. salt
- 1/8th cup packed brown sugar
- 1 tbsp. water
- 1 (3 lb.) salmon fillet
- Alder wood plank, water soaked

Directions:

1. Submerge the salmon fillet in the brine solution for 4 hours, or overnight.
2. Preheat your smoker for 160 °F
3. Remove the salmon and rinse under cold water. Dry the salmon using a paper towel. Place the fish on the plank and season with ground black pepper.
4. Place the salmon on the smoker and let smoke for 2 hours. Check at 1 ½ hours to see if the salmon is done.
5. Mix the water and brown sugar into a paste and brush onto the salmon. Allow the salmon to cook its last half hour with the brown sugar mixture. Use a fork to see if it flakes. If it flakes this means it is done.

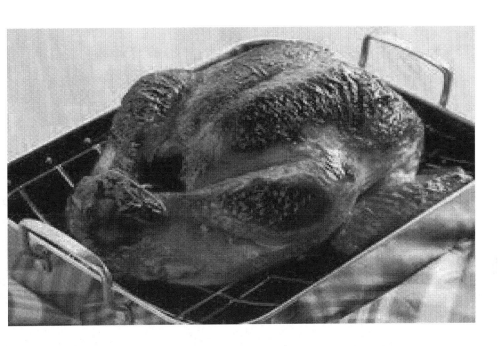

Comely Honey Turkey

(ready in about 12 hours 30 minutes | Serving 1 whole turkey)

Ingredients:

- 1 lb. salt
- 1 gallon hot water
- 2 (8 oz.) jars honey
- 2 qt. vegetable broth
- 1 (7 lb.) bag of ice
- 1 cup orange juice
- 1/4th cup vegetable oil
- 1 (15 lb.) Whole turkey, giblets and neck removed
- 1 granny smith apple, cored and cut
- 1 tsp. poultry seasoning
- 1 small onion, cut into chunks

- 1 stalk celery, cut into chunks
- 1 orange, quartered

Directions:

1. Using a large container mix salt in with water and stir until dissolved. Mix honey, vegetable broth, and orange juice. Pour the ice cubes into the brine and add the turkey afterwards so that it is breast up. Close the lid and let sit in a cold (under 40 °F) place for 12 hours.
2. Remove the turkey and dry thoroughly using a paper towel. Use a bowl to mix poultry seasoning and vegetable oil. Rub the mixture all over the turkey and place celery, apple, orange, and onion into the turkey's cavity.
3. Preheat the grill to 400 °F and place the turkey on a lightly oiled grate. Place 1 cup of the hickory wood chips to begin smoking process.
4. Grill the turkey for 1 hour on indirect heat. Check the center to see if it reaches 160 °F. Apply foil over the turkey and add more wood chips every hour cooking for an additional 2 to 3 hours. Check again for the internal temperature of 160 °F. If internal temperature has been reached, remove from the grill and let rest for 1 hour.

Conclusion

The amazing taste of smoked meat, no matter what type, gives everyone a homey feeling that can bring back amazing memories of their childhood and create new memories with friends, family and associates.

The power of smoked meat has the ability take you back to a place where you are happy, free, and comfortable. This is why you can never underestimate the power of food and the way it is cooked.

It has been proven that people are happier and more active in the summer months. Ironically, this is also when people seem to spend more time out in the sun and socializing with the people they love. It is also the time where most people break out the smokers and begin smoking meat and having barbecues.

We hope you have enjoyed the simple, yet delicious recipes that are contained in this book. The amazing flavor of each of these recipes will have you enjoying the summer, or even the winter months.

23723834R00035

Made in the USA
Middletown, DE
01 September 2015